ASTROLOGY
OF
HERBS
&
TAROT

Correspondences for Healing

LAUREN LUQUIN

For an in-depth review of my favorite tarot and oracle card decks that I use, check out my website.

Read more about Astrology, Herbs, Tarot, & other Metaphysical Tools at: www.spiralelixir.com

Lauren Luquin

Credit: The planet graphics in "Part 12 - Planetary Signatures" were custom made and designed for this book by my sister Mairin May.

Table of Contents

Preface

I wrote this book as a way to organize my thoughts, realizing that others like me may have the same interest, and perhaps by allowing the concepts to be written in a handy format, I could offer this handbook as a means to supplement my other work, and give people an opportunity to understand some of the basic correspondences between these fascinating subjects. As a teacher with a Master of Education degree in Cross-Cultural Teaching, it comes natural to me to share information, and combine knowledge from multiple perspectives and approaches, especially those that I am passionate about and have experienced first hand throughout my life.

My background in Astrology has been a life long journey and learning process, navigating my inner depths and doing intense soul work since I was a young psychic child who was drawn to and understood symbology and the spiritual realm as my first language. After having my own birth chart interpreted by Daniel Sowelu in 2009, I quickly learned how to prepare birth charts myself, and started interpreting my birth chart and progressed chart as a regular practice. I then incorporated birth chart readings into my work with family and friends, and then expanded my professional works as an Herbalist, Certified Reiki Master Teacher, Spiritual Aromatherapist and Ordained Minister & Practitioner of Metaphysics specializing in Spiritual Counseling, to offer "Cosmic Soul Maps" (in depth birth chart readings) to my clients. I've been doing tarot readings for myself and others since 1999...

I excel at facilitating energy one-on-one with people by guiding them into deeper self-awareness, using a combination of Evolutionary Astrology, Vibrational Remedies, Strategic Guidance / Life-Coaching, Keen Intuition & Psychic Awareness, Meditation, Earth Medicine, Spiritual Counseling, and various Metaphysical Tools for the mystical journey within... This handbook supplements my work, as an offering for individual discovery, self-care, and holistic wellness.

Introduction

The information contained within this handbook is intended to give practitioners and those interested in the healing arts, a convenient reference to elaborate upon one's own intuitive understanding, while highlighting important connections.

This handbook does *not* go in depth about how to create specific herbal formulas, prepare natal birth charts, or do tarot spreads for readings. Rather, it is a reference guide to expand awareness about understanding some of the correspondences between these practices. Part 12 is arranged for quick reference by planet…

This work inspires a movement of herbalists, astrologers, gardeners, tarot card readers, lightworkers, energy healers, practitioners of metaphysics, and other medicine people to expand in awareness of the more spiritual realms and to have a more engaged role in identifying and healing one's self and assisting others in doing the same.

Whether you are diving into your self-healing journey, going through a personal transformation, or helping others discover their potential within, this handbook will be helpful to you. <u>Astrology of Herbs & Tarot: Correspondences for Healing</u>, guides you to examine the interconnections between pathways of healing available to us all now.

Astrology, Herbs, and Tarot unites some of the oldest traditions, while encouraging an awareness of the ways these same methods of insight and healing are open to each of us every day.

Part 1 - How It Works

By reading through these pages from beginning to end there will be much knowledge gained, however this handbook is also intended to serve as a reference guide for practitioners of the healing arts and individuals interested in expanding awareness of self-care practices, while finding inspiration for healing with intention and confidence.

Examples:

• A woman who reads tarot cards wants to expand her clients' understanding of the interpretation, so she references this handbook for insights about how herbs correspond with the cards.

• A man who interprets birth charts for people is curious about the patterns that keep arising in regard to physical illness his clients are experiencing. He uses this handbook to understand the connections between planets and parts of the body and the chakra system, and then translates this guidance to his client in a holistic way. He's able to offer ideas about how to incorporate color therapy into their life, and suggests crystals and minerals to work with.

• A woman who enjoys gardening and cooking, becomes interested in deepening her self-awareness and learning ways to integrate self-care practices into her life, refers to this handbook as she expands on themes in her life, and makes sense of how herbs correspond with aspects of her healing journey.

• A yoga teacher, likes to recite an affirmation before his classes with his students. He draws a tarot card before each class to tune in with himself and the energy of the group, and then uses the associated affirmation to begin the lesson, charging the space with positive energy and good intentions for all present.

Part 2 - Astrology Terms

Elements / Seasons

Four states of being or states of consciousness that serve as models for physical and metaphysical processes in our lives.

Fire: Aries, Leo, Sagittarius (vernal equinox)
• developing courage; calming impulsive behavior; following through on projects

Earth: Taurus, Virgo, Capricorn (winter solstice)
• learning patience; self-discipline; hard work & taking risks to succeed

Air: Gemini, Libra, Aquarius (autumnal equinox)
• developing alertness; clarity of perception & humbling intellectual reactions

Water: Pisces, Cancer, Scorpio (summer solstice)
• learning unconditional love; fine-tuning psychic & intuitive reception

Qualities / Modes

Three archetypal phases of life cycle changes…

Cardinal: Aries, Cancer, Libra, Capricorn
• birth; the beginning of a cycle; initiation

Fixed: Taurus, Leo, Scorpio, Aquarius
• continuity; maturity; solidarity; unresponsive

Mutable: Gemini, Virgo, Sagittarius, Pisces
• the final step; ending of a cycle; adaptability

Houses of the Zodiac

A cycle of 12 symbols that represent basic human processes and fields of activity. Each house covers terrain in our life journey that is identified and made visable by taking action and experiencing life.

1st House: Personality, Self Image, Self Expression, Indentity, Masks
2nd House: Money, Values, Material Security, Self Esteem, Resources
3rd House: Communication, Learning, Speaking, Writing, Thinking
4th House: Home, Roots, Family, Heritage, Psychological Foundation
5th House: Children, Play, Fun, Pleasure, Creativity, Entertainment
6th House: Service, Duty, Self-Improvement, Work Routines, Health
7th House: Marriage, Partnerships, Alliances & Conflicts with Others
8th House: Death, Transformation, Rebirth, Renewal, Sex, Growth
9th House: Long Journeys, Searching for Meaning, Mind Expansion
10th House: Career, Public Life, Recognition, Authorities, Guides
11th House: Friends, Groups, Global Awareness, Collective Ideals
12th House: Transcendence, Sacrifice, Withdrawal, Unexpressed Self

Part 3 - The Planets

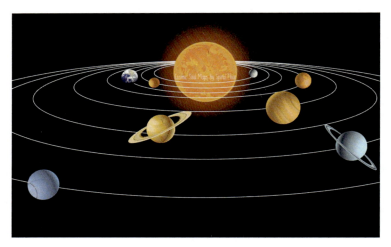

Each of the planets in our solar system have a unique personality, symbolizing certain parts of human consciousness. Every Astrological Birth Chart contains all 10 planetary signatures, but each individual's chart emphasizes different planets in different ways, and we all have free will- a choice on how to express them...

The planets represent and show us like guides what can be revealed about issues we need to learn about and evolve through in our lifetime, as well as gifts we have that we can learn to embody and utilize more fully. It is up to us to look at our birth chart, and to open our self up to what the planets are guiding us to see and experience within ourselves. We have to be willing to face the truth of our chart to change and grow in the direction of our soul's intention.

Although the Sun and Moon are not "planets" they are included with Mercury, Venus, Mars, Jupiter, Saturn, Uranus, Nepune, and Pluto.

Part 4 - Zodiac Signs

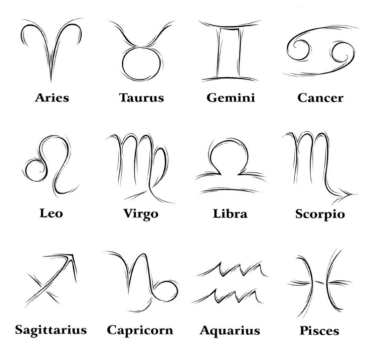

Aries	Taurus	Gemini	Cancer
Leo	Virgo	Libra	Scorpio
Sagittarius	Capricorn	Aquarius	Pisces

The 12 signs of the zodiac are evolutionary methods. No one is simply their Sun sign (the most commonly addressed sign of astrology). All of us can relate to the psychological processes represented by each sign in varying degrees. Each person is a synthesis of all 12 signs.

Each sign represents a personality type, of a universal theme.

All of the signs weave together, and can be interpreted differently depending on where each planet is located in someone's birth chart. What house it is in, and what planets it is close to all influence the energy of the planet and how it may be expressed in real life situtations. Learning about the 12 signs is a process of learning the langauage of symbology. It is tempting to simplify ourselves to "be like a Scorpio" for example, but it is much more complex than that.

Part 5 - Herbal Alchemy

The use of plants in medicine and magic have been effective for tens of thousands of years. Our ancestors' survival depended on the ways they cultivated awareness of the complex systems of information that the natural world contained around them. From observing the flow of energy in the Earth's cycles, the movement of the planets in the sky dancing with the stars, and the illuminating phases of the moon- ancient peoples were able to make wise predictions and decisions dependent on weather changes, harvesting methods, and matters of the Spirit.

Each plant contains a spiritual energy. Many medicinal plants are valued for the ability to heal and alleviate physical, emotional, mental, and spiritual conditions. The energy of plants can be embraced to bring healing and understanding to individuals and situations in intentional ways.

Plants are classified in terms of plantae kingdoms (divisions, families, etc.), form, color, climate where it grows, time of day it blooms, best gathering times, taste, smell, effect on the body systems, and ailments they address. In short, the use of Herbal Alchemy requires a plethora of information, an intuitive practice, and a transformative intention.

Combining wisdom of the cycles of the natural world with the healing properties, growth patterns, and knowledge of herbs' effectiveness in varying capacities is one way someone who is in tune and aware of the universe, may tap into the alchemy of transforming lives and purifying the Spirit. The highest intention of practicing Herbal Alchemy is to advance consciousness and expand intuitive insight to unite the Spiritual Self with respect for the plants, environmental impact, symbiotic relationships within the ecosystem, and the voices of the voiceless.

Part 6 - Blending Formulas

For most of the goals you are working toward in your life, or if the intention is to assist another person in reaching theirs, it is most effective to combine the energies of several "signatures" to reach the result one desires. A synergistic blend or union, of Astrology, Herbs and Tarot, may combine other energetic correspondences like, color-therapy, crystals, minerals, essential oils, numerology, awareness of the chakra system, and anatomical/physiological body parts, and more…

A medicinal formula is determined by first analyzing and realizing what the intention or goal is of the person, and then having awareness of the various energy correspondences for each planet.

Below is a list of ideas for combining some or many of the energy signature qualities contained in this handbook. After creating one or more of these formulas, they can then be combined to create a custom vibrational remedy or unique ceremonial experience.

Types of Custom Formulas

1. tea
2. potpourri
3. ritual oil
4. incense
5. dream pillow
6. flower essence
7. altar
8. soap
9. candle
10. essential oil blend
11. body oil
12. bath salt
13. amulet
14. elixir
15. medicine bag
16. meal
17. spritzer
18. lotion

Types of Intentional Formulas

Depending on each person, intention, and circumstance, there will be formulas to help balance, restore, enhance, expand and/or heal... Some formulas could be for a specific planet or element, others could be more complex and contain a custom intention for manifesting, like these listed below:

1. fertility
2. courage
3. dream recall
4. letting go
5. grounding
6. protection
7. abundance
8. confidence
9. prosperity
10. karma
11. love
12. career
13. self-expression
14. past lives
15. friendship

Part 7 - The Major Arcana

The most recognizable correspondences between Astrology and Tarot occur in the Major Arcana, which translates to the "Greater Secrets" cards… or what Carl Jung called, the "Major Archetypes". They are the 22 cards of the normal 78-card deck. The Minor Arcana's 56 cards also correspond to astrology and herbs, but in a much more subtle way that is dependent on a variety of factors. For this short handbook, we are gazing upon the Major Arcana, as they depict the "Big Picture" and reveal the most important, life-changing events, opportunities and experiences.

Regardless of how someone was raised and socially conditioned through family and cultural background, every human being experiences the 22 universal archetypes within their lifetime, in an array of areas of life and self. The Major Arcana's cosmic stereotypes transcend time and space, as they are universal principles that guide one to deepen, expand, grow and evolve.

Tarot decks have 4 suits, each representing an area of life. Each suit contains 10 numbered cards and 4 court (face) cards that correspond to an element, which also correspond to the planets and signs of the zodiac, etc.

The 4 Traditional Suits:

Wands = Fire
Cups = Water
Swords = Air
Pentacles = Earth

The 22 Traditional Major Arcana Cards:

0. The Fool
1. The Magician
2. The High Priestess
3. The Empress
4. The Emperor
5. The Hierophant
6. The Lovers
7. The Chariot
8. Justice
9. The Hermit
10. Wheel of Fortune

11. Strength
12. The Hanged Man
13. Death
14. Temperance
15. The Devil
16. The Tower
17. The Star
18. The Moon
19. The Sun
20. Judgment
21. The Universe

Each deck may contain different names for the suits and cards, as these days, esoteric and oracle decks are very unique, however each Major Arcana will have 4 types of suits relating to the traditional categories, and each numbered card and court card will represent the traditional classification.

For example, the common card name for the 12th Major Arcana card is "Hanged Man", but that may offend some people, or not apply to the energy of the deck, so it could be renamed as "Suspended Person", "Reversal", or the "The Mirror" card. An other example is of the "Magician" card. It may be changed to the "Witch", "Shaman", or "Gatherer" card depending on the intention of the deck.

Likewise, the 4 suits may be called various names in place of the most common. Instead of "Swords", you may see this suit called, "Arrows", or "Blades". Or the "Wands" suit may be called, "Bows", or "Flames".

Part 8 - Color

Color is linked to all aspects of our lives. We all have changing opinions about color. Colors affect our physical, emotional, spiritual, and mental conditions, so we should learn to use them to enhance our lives and heal.

Light creates color and form. Everything we see is created from reflected light. The color spectrum has hundreds of shades and variations...

Our body responds to different colors and the auric light that surrounds us varies in shades of color.

Everything in life has a vibration. Vibration exists in all things, but animate objects have a more active frequency than inanimate things. Our bodies have many energy fields. As you learn about these fields of color energy, strive to find out which energies, combinations and intensities are most effective in your healing process.

If something irritates our body's system it disrupts the vibration and we must restore balance. Vibrational remedies can do this by stabilizing the body's spiritual, emotional, physical, and mental conditions. Some of the best and most effective vibrational remedies are contained within aromas, flowers, crystals, gem stones, essences, sounds, thoughts, and COLOR.

Chromotherapy Techniques:

Chromotherapy (color-therapy) is a method of treatment that uses the color spectrum to heal dis-ease in the body*mind*spirit. There are many techniques that practitioners use to help restore balance in and heal the body. Some of them include:

- Directing colored light toward parts of the body that need healing

- Visualizing colors being inhaled by the person needing healing or restoration

- Charging colored crystals and gemstones in water by placing it in the sun and then drinking the water

- Eating various foods of certain colors

- Wearing different colored clothes

- Painting rooms in your home different colors

- Keeping objects of different colors in certain places where you see them often

The more you know about colors and the corresponding centers of the body, the easier it is to bring color into your life in healing ways. Awareness of the correlations between the planets, herbs, and chakras, helps to make decisions about what colors are needed or not. Sometimes an over abundance of a color can be making an impact. It goes both ways. Needing more of color or less, depends on how one is feeling, and what is going on holistically in someone's life.

Part 9 - Chakras

There are hundreds of energy centers in our body called chakras. Chakra (cakram) is a Sanskrit word meaning: "wheel" or "vortex".

There are 7 main chakras or energy centers that begin at the base of the spine (root) and up to the top of the head (crown). They are all connected energetically.

When one or more of the chakras are out of alignment or have a blockage of the life force energy rotating through them, it affects the mental, emotional, or spiritual state of being, which then can lead to physical dis-ease within the body, or some type of health condition arising in the body. Our bodies consist of not only the physical but also the mental (thoughts), emotional (feelings) and spirit (spiritual) bodies.

Each chakra has a color associated with it. The upper three chakras relate to the spiritual aspects of life, matters of spirit, and divinity. The lower three chakras relate to the physical mundane aspects of living and surviving on Earth (basic human needs like air, food, water, shelter, warmth, love, etc.). The heart chakra is the bridge between the upper and lower chakras. Chakras vibrate and radiate in all directions from the body.

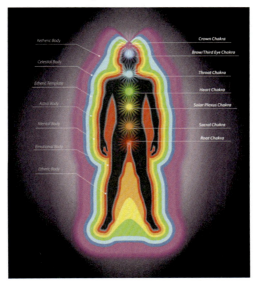

The chakras' energetic vibrations are what create the aura around the body. They are spinning energy centers that band together. After you feel comfortable getting to know colors in the outside world, go into a light state of meditation and visualize colors in your "inner world".

The 7 Main Chakras:

violet: Sahasrara: top of head - "crown"
indigo: Ajna: brow - "third eye"
blue: Vishuddha: throat
green: Anahata: heart
yellow: Manipura: solar plexus
orange: Swadisthana: navel "sacral"
red: Muladara: root

Chakras can be restored easily, as long as the intention is clear and the mind is affirming the process with positive energy.

Focus your intention and hold the vision of what you want to accomplish.

Part 10 - Affirmations

An affirmation is a positive assertion declared to be true, maintained, lived up to and dedicated to.

Affirmations help merge mental thought patterns and help you become more sensitive to the higher spiritual presence of your being.

The purpose of using affirmations is to construct your life and bring greater power to it, with which to face struggles and make your present day happier.

The power of self-belief may be your greatest help or your greatest problem.

What you believe about yourself right now, is affecting you more in this moment mentally, spiritually, emotionally, and physically, than anything else in life that you experience.

Work on changing your thoughts of lack, limitation and superficiality with truths of your spiritual mind using affirmations and creative visualization. Your True Self is Eternal and Spiritual. Be kind to yourself. Remember who you are.

Part 11 - Crystal Healing

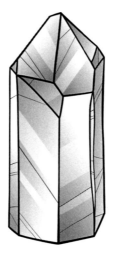

Anyone can use crystals, minerals and stones to support the healing process, as a spiritual tool. Working with crystals, minerals and stones is an intuitive process that requires focused intention to direct the healing vibrations to flow to the bodily area or chakra of a person to enhance and amplify healing.

Crystals, minerals and stones are ancient beings, that communicate and vibrate energetically. Awareness of stone medicine has been known for thousands of years throughout cultures world wide.

Natural Earth Medicine is available to us all, and yet there are in depth courses these days making it seem like something that needs to be taught, however truly, working with crystals, minerals and stones is natural to us, if we simply tune into our senses, and intuition. There are hundreds of crystals and minerals that each have healing properties, so learning about that takes time and practice, but the best way to start learning is to pick up a stone and hold it in a light state of meditation.

Collect crystals and stones that you are drawn to, and start by working with one at a time. Eventually you may use many at a time in crystal grids, laying them on your body, on your altar, carrying them together, making jewelry, or doing healing sessions for others. You can buy specimens from shops or find them in the natural world. Crystal healing correlates with colors, chakras, and intentions.

Using crystals and minerals may enhance the healing energies you're working with and help you focus the healing in specific areas, because crystals and minerals amplify the energy you're giving.

Part 12 - Energy Signatures

The Sun

Zodiac Sign:

 * Leo

<u>Colors:</u> ocher, golden hues

<u>Crystals / Minerals:</u> pyrite, pietersite, cinnabar, gold, fire opal, onyx, picture jasper

Zodiac House: 5th House

Tarot Cards & Affirmations:

* **The Sun (#19)**

"I naturally motivate others to claim their creative talent and collaborate in dynamic ways".

Strengths: creative mind, self-motivated success, innocence, curiosity, cooperative, magnetic
Challenges: removing oneself from depleting alliances, finding energizing and inspiring partnerships
Supportive Essential Oils: birch, cinnamon, ginger, lavender

* Strength (#11)
"I have unlimited creative potential and energy".

Strengths: radiant, charismatic, creative, optimistic
Challenges: self-expression, blocked energy
Supportive Essential Oils: palmarosa, fir, clary sage, jasmine

ST. JOHN'S WORT

Herbs: angelica, calendula, frankincense, chamomile, St. John's wort, juniper, rosemary, sunflower, cayenne
Tree: walnut
Chakra: third eye (pineal gland), "ajna", 6th
Parts of the Body: heart, blood circulation, body temperature

The Moon

Zodiac Sign:

* Cancer

<u>Colors:</u> white, cream, pale colors

<u>Crystals / Minerals:</u> moonstone, chalcedony, pearl, carnelian, calcite

Zodiac House: 4th House

Tarot Cards & Affirmations:

* **The High Priestess (#2)**

"I trust and value my intuition".

Strengths: looking at things in holistic ways, self-trust, sensing information
Challenges: self-criticism
Supportive Essential Oils: melissa, cypress, elemi, frankincense

* The Chariot (#7)

"I feel healthy when I balance work, play and rest".

Strengths: manifesting positive change, resourceful, focused
Challenges: overindulging, fear of failing
Supportive Essential Oils: neroli, nutmeg, chamomile roman, geranium

ALOE VERA

Herbs: anise, cabbage, cucumber, jasmine, iris, lily, lotus, mallow, mugwort, myrrh, poppy, violet, peony, cyperus
Tree: willow
Chakra: third eye (pineal gland), "ajna", 6th
Parts of the Body: eyes, bladder, breasts, brain stem, stomach, mucus membranes, parasympathetic / sympathetic nervous systems, vagina, uterus, ovaries

Mercury

Zodiac Signs:

♊ * Gemini

Colors: yellow, light green
Cyrstals & Minerals: howlite, jade, serpentine

♍ * Virgo

Colors: indigo, dark violet, silver
Cyrstals & Minerals: peridot, sugilite, snowflake obsidian, garnet, amazonite

Zodiac Houses: 3rd (Gemini) & 6th House (Virgo)

Tarot Cards & Affirmations:

* **The Magician (#1)**

"I create abundance and healing when I communicate my truth clearly".

Strengths: creative transformation through communication and divine timing
Challenges: holding back out of fear of failing
Supportive Essential Oils: clary sage, fennel (sweet), ginger, spikenard

* **The Lovers (#6)**

"I honor my emotional needs and attract others who do the same".
Strengths: relating in all relationships, people skills, knowing how to expand or let go of relationships
Challenges: following through on important choices about relationships
Supportive Essential Oils: rose, neroli, palmarosa, geranium

* **The Hermit (#9)**

"I enjoy time spent in meditation alone."
Strengths: introspective, philosophical, wise, contemplative, completing activities
Challenges: critical of self and others
Supportive Essential Oils: myrtle, neroli, pine, helichrysum

MARJORAM

Herbs: bergamot, cardomon, cinnamon, cloves, dill, hyssop, lavender, licorice, marjoram, mullien, peppermint, star anise, thyme, astragalus, parsley, licorice root

Tree: white sandalwood

Chakra: throat, thyroid gland, "visuddha", 5th

Parts of the Body: ears, hands, arms, central nervous system, sciatic nerve, left hemisphere of brain, temporal lobe

Venus

Zodiac Signs:

 * Taurus

Colors: green, brown, turquoise
Crystals / Minerals: selenite, rose quartz, rhodonite, red jasper

 * Libra

Colors: pink, light blue
Crystals / Minerals: chrysoprase, prehnite,
rose quartz, lepidolite

Zodiac Houses: 2nd House (Taurus) & 7th House (Libra)

Tarot Cards & Affirmations:

* The Empress (#3)

"I give and receive love wisely".

Strengths: giving and receiving love, deep love

Challenges: unclear priorties, sorrow, self-abandonment

Supportive Essential Oils: coriander, black pepper, melissa, neroli

* The Hierophant (#5)

"I have faith in my life and honor the sacred within me and others".

Strengths: spiritual teachings bringing the light, teaching wisdom

Challenges: anxiety, fear of rejection

Supportive Essential Oils: cedarwood, melissa, neroli, vetiver

* Justice (#8)

"When I see through illusion, I restore simplicity and healing in my life".

Strengths: honesty, centeredness, direct communication

Challenges: self-doubt, over-analyzing, over-extending oneself to others leading to depletion (burnout)

Supportive Essential Oils: orange, nutmeg, ylang ylang, patchouli

LEMON VERBANA

Herbs: blackberry, burdock, coriander, damiana, lemon verbena

Trees: alder, apple, peach, plum, cherry

Chakra: heart, "anahata", 4th

Parts of the Body: adrenal glands, tongue, receptor cells, white blood cells, cortisol, frontal lobe of brain, nose, estrogen

Mars

Zodiac Signs:

* Aries

Colors: red

Crystals / Minerals: apache tear, citrine, kyanite, carnelian, gypsum, aventurine

Zodiac House: 1st House

Tarot Cards & Affirmations:

* **The Emperor (#4)**

"I take responsibility for my natural leadership skills.".

Strengths: courage, leadership, responsible power

Challenges: fear of unfamiliar and taking risks
Supportive Essential Oils: clove, helichrysum, peppermint, petitgrain

* The Tower (#16)
"I have the power to continuously restore myself and actualize who I am".

Strengths: internally and externally fulfilled, self-healing, healing others
Challenges: fear of failure or fear of success, delaying change
Supportive Essential Oils: orange, roman chamomile, clary sage, coriander

MILK THISTLE

Herbs: black pepper, cayenne, cumin, honesysuckle, nettle, tobacco, garlic, poppy, milk thistle
Trees / Plants: juniper, hawthorn, cactus (all varieties)
Chakra: navel, core center, "manipura", 3rd
Parts of the Body: adrenal glands, arteries, veins, muscles, main part of brain, red blood cells, adrenaline, progesterine, testosterone, testes, penis, acids

Jupiter

Zodiac Signs:

 * Sagittarius

Colors: bronze, dark blue

Crystals / Minerals: lapis lazuli, sodalite, copper, azurite, turquoise

Zodiac House: 9th House

Tarot Cards & Affirmations:

* **Wheel of Fortune (#10)**

"I am open-minded and enjoy manifesting abundance".

Strengths: flexible, resiliant, creative imagination, inspired
Challenges: fixed opinions, stuck in routine or old habits, unopeness, judgmental
Supportive Essential Oils: patchouli, rosemary, clary sage, hyssop

* Temperance (#14)

"I value and honor the creative balance of the light and the dark within my own nature".

Strengths: spiritual faith, experiencing life as an art form, integrating multiple perspectives
Challenges: fear of disappointment, anxiety
Supportive Essential Oils: geranium, jasmine, eucalyptus radiata, spikenard

BORAGO

Herbs: borage ("borago"), slippery elm, echinacea
Trees: cedar, oak, pine
Chakra: sacral, lower abdomen, "swadhishthana", 2nd
Parts of the Body: sciatic nerve, legs, intestines, bone marrow

Saturn

Zodiac Signs:

♑ * Capricorn

<u>Colors:</u> all shades of brown, orange
<u>Crystals / Minerals:</u> smokey quartz, orbicular jasper, quartzite, black tourmaline, scolecite

Zodiac House: 10th House

Tarot Cards & Affirmations:

* **The Devil (#15)**
"When I retain my sense of humor in difficult situations, I feel grounded and joyful".

Strengths: creative problem-solving, playful, sensual, stable, successful

Challenges: being overly serious, laughing at something that was once painful (sense of humor about wounding)

Supportive Essential Oils: chamomile roman, juniper, vetiver, ginger

* The Universe (#21)

"I love exploring the unknown and bringing my creative ideas and projects into form".

Strengths: integrity, expressing love, communicating respectfully, contributing to community, individuality

Challenges: clarifying of priorities, releasing old wounding, breaking limiting patterns

Supportive Essential Oils: dill, spikenard, thyme, birch

VALERIAN

Herbs: beet, comfrey, ground moss, patchouli, shepard's purse, skullcap, solomon's seal, valerian, lobelia

Trees: cypress, yew

Chakra: root, tail bone, base of spine, coccyx, "muladara", 1st

Parts of the Body: arterties, veins, nose

Uranus

Zodiac Signs:

 *Aquarius

<u>Colors:</u> electric blue, silvery grey,
flourescent colors
<u>Crystals / Minerals:</u> hematite, angelite, mica
(in muscovite), ammonite, amber

Zodiac House: 11th House

Tarot Cards & Affirmations:

* **The Fool (#0)**
"I respect my true nature… I am who I am".

Strengths: courageous, risk-taking, sense of wonder
Challenges: letting go of fear, trust
Supportive Essential Oils: bay, melissa, myrrh, chamomile roman

* The Star (#17)
"When I communicate directly with clarity, I am recognized by others".

Strengths: confidence, charismatic, creative, innovative
Challenges: low self-esteem, inflating and deflating self and others, arrogance, hungry for fame
Supportive Essential Oils: linden blossom, ylang ylang, pine, grapefruit

ALLSPICE

Herbs: allspice, chicory, cloves, coffee, guarana, elemi, nutmeg, calamus, cinnamon, skullcap, ginseng
Tree: rowan
Chakra: root, tail bone, base of spine, coccyx, "muladara", 1st
Parts of the Body: central nervous system, left hemisphere of the brain, frontal lobe, sciatic nerve, brain stem

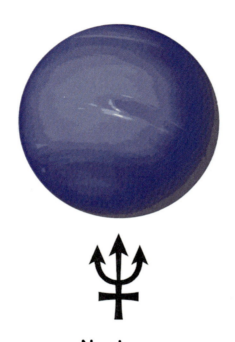

Neptune

Zodiac Signs:

 * Pisces

<u>Colors:</u> mauve, purple, aquamarine
<u>Crystals / Minerals:</u> flourite, bloodstone,
blue lace agate, aquamarine, amethyst, shells

Zodiac House: 12th House

Tarot Cards & Affirmations:

* **The Hanged Man (#12)**

"I trust the deep spiritual wisdom within me that wants to be expressed".

Strengths: integrity, self-love, open to change, acceptance of what is, moving forward
Challenges: breaking old limiting patterns, past wounding, unresolved hang-ups, ego death
Supportive Essential Oils: lemongrass, marjoram, clary sage, cypress

* The Moon (#18)

"When I go inward and explore the essence of who I am, I find happiness, strength and unlimited abundance".

Strengths: introspective, receptive, intuitive, helping others reveal authentic expression
Challenges: self-delusion, self-critical, self-judgement
Supportive Essential Oils: frankincense, rose, jasmine, juniper

Lotus

Herbs: cannabis, kava kava, mugwort, wisteria, lemon balm, skullcap, wild lettuce, lotus, neroli, sea kelp
Trees: ash
Chakra: sacral, lower abdomen, "swadhishthana", 2nd
Parts of the Body: kidneys, spleen, frontal lobe, brain stem

Pluto

Zodiac Signs:

 * Scorpio

Colors: black, red, charcoal grey
Crystals / Minerals: rhodochrosite, unakite, malachite, labradorite, charoite

Zodiac House: 8th House

Tarot Cards & Affirmations:

* **Death (#13)**
"When I let go with dignity I become more of who I am".

Strengths: teaching and modeling letting go, experiencing depth in relationships, transformation and change
Challenges: feeling incomplete, letting go of attachments
Supportive Essential Oils: myrrh, lemon, neroli, cardamon

* Judgment (#20)

"I observe people and situations and communicate what I see in a way others receive well".

Strengths: self-trust, perceptive, insightful, inner peace, resourceful, utilizing good judgment, constructive criticism
Challenges: communicating perceptions in a way others understand, being objective
Supportive Essential Oils: sandalwood, neroli, oakmoss, juniper

NETTLE

Herbs: barley, black cohosh, corn, damiana, oats, saw palmetto, wheat, elder, goldenseal, patchouli, wormwood, saw palmetto, nettle
Trees / Fungi: maple, fly agaric, psilocybin
Chakra: navel, core center, "manipura", 3rd
Parts of the Body: adrenal glands, ateries, veins, penis, testes, vagina, estrogen, stomach, ovaries, breasts, uterus, mucus membranes, anal canal

Conclusion

Astrology of Herbs & Tarot is a handbook that offers an opening to a process through which creative interpretation and intuitive guidance can be gently guided with suggestions of correspondences between multiple concepts for healing and invoking spiritual power and awareness. Use it as a quick reference when drawing your own conclusions. It's meant to be convenient and helpful as you dive into exploring many more correlations that may arise.

Therapeutic options and associations made in this handbook should not be used as a tool to determine exactly which herb, or color must be paired with each physical symptom... Rather, we all should tune in with our own innate authority and make our own connections. Using the information within these pages may be of inspiration and also a nudge to explore each of the subjects covered in more depth. The more someone knows about herbs for example, the more one can bring that dimension into their healing journey and make sense of the correspondences.

Sometimes there are overlaps in the correspondences, and that's because Astrology, Herbs, Tarot, and the other concepts covered in this handbook are not fixed entities stuck in a rigid framework. Each of us has our own interpretation and healing journey, and each topic in this handbook is full of potential, open to be explored and filled with multiple healing properties.

Spiral Elixir provides messages for the spiritual alchemist's path and tools for the journey within. May we all share what we know best about divine connection to help everyone integrate a more complete spiritual experience, as we shape and weave the fabric of everyday reality. We are the conscious co-creators of this life. The collective mind. Tune In, Be Aware of Oneness, Open in Perception, Grateful for it all. Expand your awareness of the concepts in this handbook with Lauren's advanced level course and other works at her website.

If you're interested in gaining more insights about your personal astrological birth chart, having a reading to explore the tarot together, or are curious about how to use this handbook in association with a Transformational Healing Session or Intuitive Psychic Reading, please contact Lauren Luquin at lauren@spiralelixir.com for a free consultation.

Download her *free* eBook, Essential Oil Blends: A Beginner's Guide at her website, www.spiralelixir.com.

About the Author

Lauren Luquin is a multi-disciplinary artist and practitioner. Her practice stems from her childhood awareness and inner evolution throughout her life, mixed with professional training and education. Her degrees & credentials include: Usui Reiki Master Teacher, Certified Spiritual Aromatherapist, Bachelor of Metaphysical Science, Ordained Minister & Practitioner of Metaphysics - Spiritual Counseling, Master of Education in Cross-Cultural Teaching, California State Multiple-Subject Teaching Credential: grades K-12, Bachelor of Arts in Sociology...

Owner of Spiral Elixir since 2004, the intention of her work is to honor the Inner Divine and Universal Consciousness by highlighting the many ways that we can uncover our True Eternal Self as we balance the light and dark & musculine/feminine within and without. Her website www.spiralelixir.com is an accumulation of offerings for inspiration and contemplation, as well as a portal for accessing heightened levels of consciousness to strengthen the connection we each have with the whole.

Our individual light is needed to evolve the Universal Spirit of Nature, and Spiral Elixir works to support this inner journey of discovery and transmutation of the True Self- by supporting the process of successfully integrating the inner and the outer, dealing with the shadow aspects with attention and healing, transcending the limitations of the ego, and fostering creative community with other seekers. Spiral Elixir is dedicated to Transformational Healing & Empowerment.

Lauren is a Scorpio Sun, Taurus Moon, and Pisces Rising. She was born 11-11-1981 in San Diego, CA - USA and now lives in the Sierra Nevada Foothills in Northern California near the Yuba River. She has been married for over 10 years and has 2 children. For more information read her Bio at her website... www.spiralelixir.com/about-lauren-luquin/

Stay connected...

Follow on Instagram @spiralelixir

Like on Facebook @spiralelixir

Be sure to sign up for Lauren's free newsletter as well...

Spiral Elixir Newsletter Sign Up Page

Made in the USA
Middletown, DE
21 October 2016